DATE DUE			

92
MEN
Brill, Marlene Targ
Journey for Peace: The story of
Rigoberta Menchu

11-139
$14.99

DEMCO

Journey for Peace

Also by Marlene Targ Brill

Allen Jay and the Underground Railroad

Extraordinary Young People

Guatemala

Let Women Vote!

Trail of Tears

Journey for Peace
THE STORY OF RIGOBERTA MENCHÚ

by MARLENE TARG BRILL
illustrated by Rubén De Anda

A RAINBOW BIOGRAPHY

LODESTAR BOOKS

Dutton   New York

Library of Congress Cataloging-in-Publication Data

Brill, Marlene Targ.
    Journey for peace: the story of Rigoberta Menchú / by Marlene Targ Brill; illustrated by Rubén De Anda.—1st ed.
        p.   cm.—(A Rainbow biography)
    Includes bibliographical references and index.
    ISBN 0-525-67524-8 (alk. paper)
    1. Menchú, Rigoberta—Juvenile literature.   2. Quiché women—Biography—Juvenile literature.   3. Human rights workers—Guatemala—Biography—Juvenile literature.
4. Mayas—Civil rights—Juvenile literature.   5. Mayas—Government relations—Juvenile literature.   6. Guatemala—Politics and government—Juvenile literature.   7. Guatemala—Ethnic relations—Juvenile literature.   8. Menchú, Rigoberta.
I. De Anda, Rubén, 1945–   . II. Title. III. Series.
F1465.2.05M383   1996
972.81′004974—dc20
[B]   95-36741
                                                                    CIP

Published in the United States by Lodestar Books,
an affiliate of Dutton Children's Books,
a division of Penguin Books USA Inc.,
375 Hudson Street, New York, New York 10014

Published simultaneously in Canada
by McClelland & Stewart, Toronto

Editor: Rosemary Brosnan   Designer: Marilyn Granald

Printed in the U.S.A.   First Edition
10 9 8 7 6 5 4 3 2

to Rigoberta Menchú
and children everywhere who
believe in peace and justice

Acknowledgments

Many people helped me learn about Rigoberta Menchú and Guatemala. I want to thank María Vázquez, the Vicente Menchú Foundation; The Norwegian Nobel Institute; Arturo Arias, San Francisco State University; Tom Kolze, Guatemalan News and Information Bureau; Kara Hooper, Peace Brigades International; Meredith Sommers, Resource Center of the Americas; Marc Zimmerman, University of Illinois; and John Parenteau. Special thanks to Lucretia Oliva, Organization of Solidarity with the People of Guatemala, and her daughter, Alejandra Cabrera, for their thoughtful reading of the book.

Contents

Map of Guatemala   viii

Introduction: Symbol of Peace   1

1   Child of the Land   4

2   Child Worker   12

3   Call for Change   18

4   The Hunted   28

5   Hidden Voice from Mexico   34

6   Dreams of Peace   41

Endnotes   47

Glossary   49

Further Reading   51

Index   53

INTRODUCTION

Symbol of Peace

Rigoberta Menchú stood proudly on the open back of a pickup truck. Four strong bodyguards encircled her. Their eyes searched the crowds for danger as the beat-up truck crept along. But Rigoberta showed no fear. The gentle woman in brightly colored dress just smiled and waved.

Rigoberta Menchú rarely returned to Guatemala from her hiding place in Mexico. When she did, the short, dark-haired woman carefully slipped into town so soldiers could not find and arrest her. The Guatemalan army had branded her an enemy. They tried to stop her from talking about government violence against her family and the Mayan people.

Today was special, however. Well-wishers lined the dusty streets of San Marcos, Guatemala, five miles from where the thirty-three-year-old woman had been born. Church bells rang. Mayan Indians poured from their homes. Women openly offered Rigoberta gifts from the earth—flowers, fruits, and

1

Rigoberta Menchu celebrated her 1992 Nobel Peace Prize in the streets of San Marcos, Guatemala. (AP/Wide World)

vegetables. They cheered the woman who had just received the 1992 Nobel Peace Prize.

Poor Guatemalans throughout the country rejoiced at the news. The Nobel Peace Prize was famous around the world. Rigoberta Menchú was one of their own, and her winning the prize gave Mayan Indians hope. Maybe people would listen and help native Guatemalans now. Perhaps the kidnapping, torture, and killing of Indians could end.

Rigoberta Menchú called for the truck to stop. The crowd quieted to hear her speak. Rigoberta thanked the brave people who had come to see her. Then she vowed to end the silence about how the Guatemalan government mistreated her people. As Nobel Peace Prize winner, she would tell the world of her hard life. She would tell the story of all Native Americans who struggle to live in peace.

ONE

Child of the Land

Rigoberta Menchú's story began in the altiplano, the high northwest mountains of Guatemala. Her family's thatched-roof home nestled in the shaded forests around Chimel, a beautiful but poor new village. Vicente and Juana Menchú, Rigoberta's parents, had built this tiny hideaway before their daughter was born.

The family had once lived on a small strip of land they owned in the province of El Quiché. But they hardly earned enough money to eat. Greedy land-lords took parts of their farm to pay the family's bills. Soon rich landowners forced Rigoberta's parents from their home and farther into the mountains toward Chimel.

Vicente and Juana farmed and wove mats, cloth, and *huipiles*, blouses with the village pattern, day and night. They saved enough money to buy more land in the mountains. Over time, other families joined them, and a small town appeared. The townspeople knew they had years of clearing shrubs and planting ahead of them before the earth would bear fruit. Still, they loved their overgrown mountain homes.

Rigoberta's parents and her five older sisters and brothers usually stayed only four months of the year in this wooded paradise. They collected *mimbre*, or willow cane, from the forest to sell at the city market. The rest of the year they picked coffee beans, cotton, and sugar on *fincas*, or large farms owned by a few rich men, along the coast.

In 1959 Juana barely made it back from the coffee fields before Rigoberta, her sixth child, was born. Vicente stayed on the *finca* with the older children to pick coffee beans. A midwife, Juana's parents, and the village leaders tended Rigoberta's birth. These village leaders helped with the baby to show that Rigoberta belonged to the entire village, not just to her parents.

Following Mayan custom, the midwife pierced Rigoberta's ears. Then she tied red thread around the baby's hands and feet for eight days. The ties showed that Rigoberta's body was pure and should be used only as nature planned—to work the land. These ties warned the infant always to care for the earth that gave her life.

Another piece of thread held a small red sack around Rigoberta's little neck. The sack was red to give her strength and long life, like the sun that guided all living things. It contained herbs, plants,

5

and other treasures from the earth—salt, lime, tobacco, and garlic—to keep her from harm.

At forty days, Rigoberta's family took her to a special celebration. In front of the entire village, her parents promised to teach her the secrets of the Mayan people. Village leaders shared stories they had been told about Indians of long ago.

They recalled the days when strangers from Spain invaded their land. They prayed to Father Sun and Mother Moon: "Let no landowner or rich person wipe out our customs. Let this child keep our secrets of life as her grandparents lived."[1]

And so Rigoberta began her childhood—steeped in the Mayan traditions of her ancestors. From her earliest days, she learned how she sprang from the earth like maize and beans, and how she must always love the earth and follow the ways of her people.

As a young child, Rigoberta's happiest times were with her family in the mountains. Their closest neighbors were miles down the rugged slopes by foot. But Rigoberta was too busy to miss her friends.

Each morning the little girl awoke before sunrise. Everybody had a job to finish before breakfast. Rigoberta's older brothers gathered wood for a cooking fire, while her younger brother, Petrocinio, picked the few vegetables that grew in the garden. Rigoberta fed corncobs to the dogs that guarded the seedlings. Her older sister carried water from a far-away stream.

Her mother ground maize into flour for the morning tortillas, or flat bread. Juana mixed the water and maize into dough. She patted the dough perfectly round and paper thin. Then she gently placed the maize pancakes on a clay plate for baking over the fire. The sweet smell was Rigoberta's signal to come for the first meal of the day.

After breakfast, Rigoberta helped plant maize and beans or cared for the hens and sheep. Some days Rigoberta and her mother trudged more than two miles to wash clothes. They scrubbed their handwoven cloth on stones in the fast-flowing stream south of Chimel. Sometimes, Rigoberta played hide-and-seek in the woods with children who also came to wash clothes with their mothers. Other times, she looked for mushrooms to sell at the village market for a few centavos.

Rigoberta especially liked to help her father. Vicente was a village leader and the person Rigoberta admired most. Rigoberta followed him everywhere—into the thicket to cut shrubs and into the forest to clear logs and brush for a garden.

One day Vicente called for seven-year-old Rigoberta and the older children. He told them the family had no money for food. Their baby brother and sister were too sick for the long trip to the *finca*, so the family couldn't go there to work.

"The only thing for us to do is go up the mountain and collect *mimbre*," he said sadly. "I will sell the willow branches in the city."[2]

The children said good-bye to their mother and the babies. Darkness closed in around them as Vicente and the family guide dog led them higher up the mountain. The tall trees were so thick with leaves that they covered the forest with endless nighttime. Only the sweet songs of birds filled the cool mountain air.

That night Rigoberta slept on the cold, hard ground. Forest animals howled and yelped. The scared girl wrapped a shawl tightly over her head to block out the sounds.

The next day Rigoberta gathered whatever long branches her tiny arms could carry. She lugged

one or two at a time and added them to the pile
collected by her brothers and sisters. A small mound
in the clearing grew bigger each day. Vicente tied
bunches of *mimbre* with rope to drag home.

After a week, Rigoberta noticed that their dog
had disappeared. The food ran out, so Vicente said
that they had better leave too. But he was unsure of
the path back without the dog. He warned the children to stay together. They had a long hike back
and didn't want to meet any bears or coyotes.

Vicente went first to clear a path through the forest. The children fell into a line behind him, pulling
piles of *mimbre*. Rigoberta tried to keep her place at
the end of the line but soon trailed the others.

Vicente went down one wrong path after another to find the trail back home. The longer they walked, the farther behind Rigoberta dropped. She called to her brothers and sisters. But they were too far away to hear.

Rigoberta grew cold and hungry. She wandered through the forest alone. Maybe a bear will eat me, worried the scared girl.

When Vicente noticed Rigoberta was gone, he became crazy with worry. He retraced their steps for seven hours. At last they found Rigoberta. Everyone blamed her for being so careless.

I must be more responsible, more like my brothers and sisters, Rigoberta thought.[3]

The family plodded through the rain-soaked forest for three more days without food. They tore parts of palm plants and ate them. Little by little, they unloaded bits of soggy *mimbre*. Finally, Vicente saw their dog—they had found the village.

Rigoberta went with Vicente to Guatemala City, the country's capital, to sell what *mimbre* was left. This was her first trip on a truck with windows. Initially, Rigoberta was afraid to ride. But the sight of towns, mountains, and houses speeding by quickly pushed aside her fears.

"What are those strange animals on the road?" Rigoberta asked her father when they reached the city. "They are cars," he answered. "We take trucks to carry things. Cars belong to rich people to use just for themselves."[4]

Vicente and Rigoberta took their load to a furniture maker who usually bought *mimbre* from villagers. At first the man refused to buy the *mimbre*.

Vicente begged the man to change his mind. The city was strange to him. He spoke only Quiché, the language of his village. Most city people were ladinos—children of Mayan and Spanish parents—or Mayas who rejected their native heritage and spoke Spanish.

The man seemed to laugh at her father. Finally, he agreed to buy the *mimbre*, but at half price. Rigoberta had never seen her father so upset.

For the first time, she understood how really poor they were. She saw how terribly ladinos treated her people. Rigoberta and her family had suffered a week of cold, rain, and hunger for twenty-five Guatemalan quetzals, less than four U.S. dollars and seventy-five cents!

"The city for me that day was a monster," Rigoberta wrote later. "Those houses, those people. This was the world of ladinos. We were different."[5]

Vicente saw Rigoberta's sadness. On the ride home, he told her that life would get better. He said that he had already talked with leaders of other villages about the need for change. He would take more trips to plan ways of improving the living conditions of Mayan children. Then he lowered his voice. "When you are old enough, you must travel around the country. You must do what I do."[6]

TWO

Child Worker

Rigoberta's earliest travels were to the *finca*. She and her family boarded a dirty flatbed truck whenever they needed money for food. A driver from the *finca* stuffed Rigoberta and about forty other workers into the canvas-covered back.

Families brought mats to sleep on, cooking pots, and their dogs, cats, and chickens. The driver stopped to get out and stretch. Everyone else had to stay on the truck—sometimes for two bumpy nights and a day—without time to stand or relieve themselves. The smell from animals and too many people squeezed together often made Rigoberta sick.

Rigoberta liked the *finca* even less than the truck ride. Bosses with guns herded them into a large open hut without sides. As many as four hundred men, women, and children lived under its leaf-covered roof during harvest. They had no running water or walls to separate families. Flies and filth

were everywhere. With the noise and jumble of hundreds of Indians speaking different Mayan languages, Rigoberta could hardly sleep.

At first, Rigoberta helped care for her younger brother and sister. That way, her mother could pick coffee beans faster. By age eight Rigoberta earned money of her own. She never attended school. Instead, she weeded and picked coffee beans from three in the morning until sundown with only a short midday break for food.

Her pay was twenty centavos (about four U.S.

cents) a day to pick thirty-five pounds of coffee. If a branch broke and damaged the bush, she earned less money. Rigoberta learned to pluck the small beans gently from their branches.

Bosses forced everyone to pick their share, or they worked the next day without pay. Rigoberta tried hard to keep up. Her little body often ached from sunburn and constant bending to gather beans that fell under the coffee bushes.

One day Rigoberta was so hot and tired she fell asleep under a bush. When she awoke, she struggled to pick her share before sunset. By seven o'clock her brothers and sisters offered to help.

"I must learn for myself," Rigoberta told them firmly.[7]

The worst part of the *finca* for Rigoberta was the pain and suffering she saw around her. Landowners rarely gave workers enough food. Often her family ate rotten tortillas and beans. Without good food, many children grew sick or died.

Workers could buy more food at the landowner's farm store. But prices were high, and the landowner subtracted money from their small pay. After a month's work, Rigoberta's mother and father sometimes owed the landowner more than they had earned. Workers who complained lost their jobs and the ride back home.

On one trip to the *finca*, Rigoberta's brother Nicolás became sick. The two-year-old cried most of the next fifteen days. Rigoberta's mother fed

Nicolás many different plants to try to cure him. Still, his stomach swelled from lack of food.

Juana had nobody to call for help. Vicente was at another *finca*. She would lose her job if she stopped working. Most other workers were from another village and spoke a different Mayan language, and the landowner spoke only Spanish. She had no money for doctors or medicine. Rigoberta watched helplessly as her brother grew weaker.

Early one morning, little Nicolás stopped breathing. Rigoberta, her mother, and her brothers took a day to bury and mourn him. The boss threw them out for losing a day's work.

The family's wages went to bury the baby on the *finca*. They were many miles from Chimel without a way to return home. A few other workers from Rigoberta's village collected money to pay the landowner and send them back to the mountains.

Nicolás's death saddened and angered Rigoberta. "This is the life I will lead, too—having many children who will die."[8]

In between trips to the *finca*, Rigoberta's family and their neighbors near Chimel cleared more land for farms. For years few plants grew, and villagers were left to themselves. Then the land finally sprouted crops. Rich landowners suddenly appeared, claiming the land as theirs.

As village leader, Rigoberta's father led the protest against the rich landowners. At first, Vicente followed the law as the judges ordered. He traveled to the city at great cost to the family. He had the land measured. He put his mark on many papers even though he couldn't read or write. But few lawmakers listened to a poor Indian.

Then Vicente collected money from villages to hire lawyers to speak for him. The lawyers took the money and filed many papers with judges. But the lawyers and judges who controlled land claims received payoffs from the wealthy landowners. So the judges always gave the same answer. The Indians must move.

Rigoberta's village refused to give up, so landowners plotted to force them off the land. In 1967, the landowners hired soldiers to raid the village. Rigoberta and her family barely escaped into the rain-soaked fields. The soldiers destroyed their home and stole keepsakes that had belonged to her grandmother. They even killed the animals, which, for the Mayas, is like killing a person.

After forty days in hiding, Rigoberta's family called a meeting of the other homeless villagers. They announced that they would rather die than give up their land. From then on, the village prepared to keep landowners from scaring them off the farms.

Rigoberta and her family moved back home and helped dig up the scattered belongings they had buried for safekeeping. Indians from nearby villages brought new cooking pots and grinding stones. One of Rigoberta's parents always stayed home from the *finca* to guard their house.

Within a few months, the landowners tried a new plan. Dishonest judges sent inspectors to tell Vicente that Chimel belonged to the Indians if everyone signed a paper. Even young Rigoberta pressed her ink-stained finger where the inspector pointed. But the paper was in Spanish, so she couldn't read the words.

Two years later Rigoberta learned they had been tricked. The paper really gave the Indians only two years in their homes—long enough to clear and plant more land for the rich landowners.

Rigoberta was enraged. The Mayas worked so hard. Yet, ladinos refused to respect their customs and rights to the land.

THREE

Call for Change

Each year Rigoberta returned to the *finca* with her family. She grew taller and stronger, and she picked faster. By age twelve Rigoberta earned thirty-five centavos (about seven U.S. cents) a day for picking seventy pounds of coffee.

Then her good friend, María, died on the *finca*. A plane had sprayed the fields with bug killers while María and other Indians worked. Rigoberta remembered a similar story about an older brother. His young body had breathed too much poison, and he, too, had died.

Rich landowners don't care about the lives of poor Indians, she thought bitterly. [9]

Because Rigoberta was now twelve, her village expected her to think and act like a woman. Rigoberta's parents gave her a pig to raise. Her father began taking her with him to speak with villagers who had problems. She taught children at home and on the *finca* the lessons of her people.

María's death forced Rigoberta to think more about the cruel life ahead—the hunger, the sickness, the backbreaking work, and the rich landowners who tried to steal what little the Indians gained. She wondered what she could do to better the lives of Indians.

Rigoberta decided to learn Spanish, the language of the rich and powerful. Her problem was how. Rigoberta's family still earned too little to afford to send her to school. Even if they had the money, Vicente distrusted ladino schools.

Rigoberta's chance to learn Spanish came on her next trip to the *finca*. A landowner asked Rigoberta's father if she could be his maid in Guatemala City. She would collect twenty quetzals (about three U.S. dollars and eighty cents) a month, more than double her pay for picking coffee beans.

Vicente disapproved at first. "That's a bad life," he argued. "Look how poorly they treated your sister when she was a maid in the city." Vicente also feared Rigoberta would forget Mayan ways. Rigoberta, however, saw the job as a way to help her family and their village.

Before she turned thirteen, Rigoberta said good-bye to her mother, father, and brothers and sisters for the first time. The scared girl left the *finca* for the capital with the landowner and his guards. Rigoberta arrived at the landowner's house without shoes and with only the thin shawl, old blouse, and dirty skirt she wore while picking coffee beans.

The landowner's wife took one look at Rigoberta and ordered her taken away and scrubbed. Another Indian maid in ladino clothes showed Rigoberta where to wash. Then she led Rigoberta to a tiny room with piles of boxes and plastic bags and left. This was Rigoberta's bedroom.

The next day, the wife bought Rigoberta a cheap skirt and blouse. She told the other maid to explain that Rigoberta was always to wear the clothes in the house.

Rigoberta was shocked. She was proud of her colorful *huipil*, with its hand-sewn designs of her Quiché village. Why did this woman expect her to pay for the ladino clothes with her first two months' wages?

I need the money for my parents, thought Rigoberta, fighting back tears. But Rigoberta knew too little Spanish to argue.

Rigoberta worked without rest from seven in the morning until late at night. She swept the house and yard, washed clothes and dishes, made beds, ironed, and watered the plants. Many jobs were strange to her. She had never used a toilet or iron before or dried plates that shined.

Rigoberta tried to learn quickly. But she felt the rich woman watching her every move. Nothing pleased this spoiled woman. Rigoberta cleaned clothes and made beds over and over until the woman was satisfied. Soon, the jobs became easier, and Rigoberta learned to speak some Spanish.

The work was unusually tiring. But what both-
ered Rigoberta most was how the family treated
her. Rigoberta's bed was an uncovered mattress in a
dark, dingy room where the family stored garbage.
The landowner's sons threw things at her and
shouted orders. The rich woman called Rigoberta
lazy and said she only wanted their food. Yet, they
fed her hard tortillas and a few beans, while the
family dog ate meat and rice.

"She treats me worse than a dog," said Rigoberta
sadly.[10]

Rigoberta missed her parents. She hated the city and the rich ladinos who treated Indians like dirt. She missed the mountains and forest and ways of her village.

The homesick girl lasted for little more than eight months. By now, the woman and Rigoberta barely talked. The other maid, who had become Rigoberta's friend, left for a better job. Rigoberta wanted to leave, too, but the woman owed her two months' back pay.

Finally, the woman gave her the forty quetzals. At once, Rigoberta announced that she must leave. The woman hollered and begged her to stay. But Rigoberta ignored her as she hummed a cheerful Mayan song and prepared to go. Then Rigoberta's brother appeared at the back door looking troubled.

"Papa is in prison," he said.[11]

While Rigoberta was in the city, Vicente had traveled to villages far from Chimel and held meetings. At each gathering, he heard the same story. Everyone told of rich landowners who were trying to steal their land too.

The landowners feared what would happen if large numbers of Indians banded together. They had threatened to harm Vicente. But he remained unafraid and continued to visit other Mayas. Then the landowners had paid judges to throw him in jail.

Rigoberta and her brother rushed from the rich woman's house to the jail. They found Vicente in a

large, dirty cell with outlaws and sick men. Rigoberta knew that her father's only crime was being poor and wanting justice. She promised to work until she had money to pay educated people who could help free him.

Rigoberta returned to the *finca* with all of her brothers. They never went home that year. Every month one brother took their wages to Juana in San Juan. She added the money to what she earned as a maid. Rigoberta's family vowed to free Vicente.

Vincente was released from jail more than a year

later. But the landowners were still angry. Three months later, Rigoberta was at home when terrible news came. Landowners' guards had kidnapped and beaten her father.

Rigoberta found Vicente's battered body on the ground, where he had been left for dead. She could hardly look at him. He had several broken bones and deep cuts on his skin.

Rigoberta asked villagers to carry him to town. Landowners had already paid the doctor not to care for her father. The village priest took Vicente by truck to a hospital many miles away in Santa Cruz. There Rigoberta's mother took another job as a maid, this time to pay for medicine and doctors.

Rigoberta hated landowners and all ladinos for what they had done to her father and mother. First, they steal our land and force us to work for little pay, she cried. Now they openly kill us.[12]

Rigoberta decided to starve rather than farm ladino land. She had a baby sister to care for now. Rigoberta and her brothers and sisters decided to stay in the mountains and grow their own crops for food.

Vicente healed enough for him and Juana to come home. But Rigoberta's father was never the same again. Unending pain kept him up at night and gave him trouble walking. Still, he quickly returned to his work for Indian rights.

Rigoberta lived in constant fear for her father's life. She started going with him to different villages.

They traveled by night through hidden mountain paths to stay away from soldiers. "We must fight the rich," Vicente told his daughter. "They become rich with our land, our crops."[13]

By age fifteen, Rigoberta was an important person in her village. Her father's friends knew her. She worked with priests and outsiders from Europe who tried to help her people. She led teens' and women's classes in Bible studies and self-defense.

One day when Vicente was away the army came to Chimel. Ninety soldiers slept for fifteen days in the village meetinghouse. They cut the maize without giving thanks to Mother Earth.

The villagers did nothing to anger them. Rigoberta wore a shawl over her head so that soldiers couldn't see her angry eyes. After they left, she and her brothers called a meeting to think of a plan. They never wanted soldiers to stay and steal their food again.

Every man, woman, and child chose a job. Rigoberta helped build new houses so villagers could live closer together. She took her turn as a lookout each night.

Others gathered weapons from the earth to protect themselves—stones, lime to burn eyes, sticks, boiling water, hot chilies, and salt. They dug ditches as traps and taught the dogs to bark at strangers. Everyone learned a secret signal. Then they practiced escaping and meeting at a hiding place in the forest.

The next time soldiers surprised them, the villagers were ready. A lookout gave the signal to quietly flee. Guard dogs announced the soldiers and barked until they left.

Each time soldiers came, they searched for young Indian men to join the army. If the men wouldn't join, the soldiers killed them. But now the soldiers found only an empty village.

On one visit, the angry soldiers tore up houses and beat the dogs. Rigoberta watched from her hideaway. She longed to get back at the soldiers.

Rigoberta and her brothers quickly decided to kidnap a soldier. As the soldiers left, a pretty girl called aside one soldier, who fell behind. Rigoberta pretended to point a gun at his back. She laughed to think she could ever pull the trigger of a real gun.

The soldier turned out to be an Indian. Rather than hurt him, Rigoberta and the other women of the village scolded him and sent him back to his camp. He was to set a good example for his race.

Landowners heard that the people of Chimel were united and they stayed away. Rigoberta was happy. Her village knew how to protect itself without bloodshed. She must share what they had learned with other villages.

FOUR

The Hunted

Rigoberta Menchú began to travel as her father did. She stayed with families in other villages. They offered her bits of their food. They made space in crowded one-room huts for her to sleep next to them on the dirt floor.

As she traveled, Rigoberta noticed that many villages faced much bigger problems than Chimel did. Indians disappeared, sometimes never to be seen again. The army tortured and killed families of village leaders. They forced entire villages into guarded camps.

Rigoberta discovered that the one thing that kept Indians helpless was their language. Mayas spoke about twenty-two different languages. How could she share the secrets of her village with other Indians when she spoke only Quiché? How could Indians fight ladino laws if they could not read them in Spanish?

Rigoberta asked the families she stayed with to

teach her their language. Over the next few years she learned to speak Tzutujil, Cakchiquel, and Mam, three of the four main Mayan languages. Rigoberta also asked Catholic nuns in the villages to teach her to read and write in Spanish. Gradually, she gained what her people needed most to fight for peace and justice—a way to talk with one another and with non-Indians.

Now Rigoberta could visit towns where Mayas suffered most. She listened to their troubles. She comforted those who had lost parents, children, sisters, or brothers. She taught women how to become village leaders and how to set traps that kept soldiers from hurting them.

By 1978, everyone in Rigoberta's family was in danger. Two sisters had joined rebel groups of Indians who took up arms to protect themselves. The army regarded Rigoberta, her father, and brothers as a threat because of their work in different villages.

Soldiers had hounded Vicente ever since his beating. He was jailed many times. According to the judges, he caused unrest among the people. Three years after his beating, soldiers dragged Vicente from the house and arrested him once again. This time, judges ordered him killed for his suspected crimes.

By now, Vicente was an important leader. Rigoberta's family sent word to those who worked with him. Factory and farm laborers, students, priests, and villagers marched for his freedom. The judge let Vicente go after fifteen days. But he warned Vicente not to speak out anymore or he or his children would die.

Vicente left jail with greater courage to fight. While in the overcrowded cell, Vicente met a man who told him that all poor Guatemalans—Indian and non-Indian, factory and farmworker—have the same problems. The man urged Vicente to create a new group of those who were marching outside to free him from jail.

Vicente helped form the Committee of Peasant Unity, or CUC in Spanish. The CUC was for anyone who wanted change in Guatemala. Vicente hid in the mountains to protect his family. Secretly, he visited villages to spread the word about the power of joining CUC.

Rigoberta rarely saw any of her family. In 1978 she heard that her parents, brothers, and sisters were in Chimel, and she returned home too. Rigoberta shared the happiest days in a long time with her family.

Villagers held a special fiesta in their honor. They killed a pig to eat with tamales, maize paste wrapped in maize leaves. They cooked maize dough, water, sugar, and salt into a drink. Music filled the village meetinghouse, as people played drums, clay whistles, and marimbas late into the night.

At midnight, Vicente announced that he must leave on a job for CUC. Worried for his safety, the family said a tearful good-bye. Because the CUC was growing stronger, the government vowed to crush its leaders. Before he went, Vicente proudly turned to Rigoberta and reminded her to keep doing good for her people.

Soon after, Vicente faded into the forest. The next morning, Rigoberta, her mother, and brothers left for different villages. The fiesta was the last time Rigoberta saw her family together alive.

On September 9, 1979, five masked men with guns captured Rigoberta's sixteen-year-old brother, Petrocinio, near the village. They tied his hands behind his back and dragged him to an army camp. There soldiers beat and kicked him.

They tortured him for sixteen days. Then the army drove him and three truckloads of other prisoners to the town of Chajul. Soldiers ordered everyone from surrounding villages to come and see what happens to people who oppose them.

Rigoberta and her family sneaked into town. She wept at the sight of her brother. Rigoberta watched helplessly as soldiers threw gasoline on his scarred body and set him on fire.

Rigoberta felt rage through her tears. Petrocinio didn't deserve such pain. Nobody did.

Four months later, Vicente and other CUC members marched into Guatemala City. They protested the kidnappings, awful wages, and unfair treatment of poor Indians and ladinos. Members took over a radio station and invaded the Spanish embassy. They wanted the country and the world to know what was happening in Guatemala.

The CUC thought the army wouldn't dare bother them in the embassy. The protesters guessed wrong. The army threw bombs into the embassy that exploded, killing Vicente and thirty-seven others inside. Any hopes for peaceful change died with the men.

On April 19, 1980, soldiers grabbed Juana on her way back from buying food for starving villagers. They asked her to tell them where her children were. When she refused, the soldiers shaved her head and beat her to death.

Rigoberta's heart ached for her mother and

father. For the first time, her sadness made her want to die. Then she remembered her father's request for her to continue his work.

Rigoberta decided to fight those who had hurt her family. She would follow her father's footsteps in CUC. Somehow she would tell the world how much poor Guatemalans had suffered.

FIVE

Hidden Voice from Mexico

Rigoberta headed for the coast to talk with coffee and cotton pickers. She hurried from *finca* to *finca*, staying just long enough to share what she had learned elsewhere. Then she returned to the mountains. She met with farmworkers, factory workers, and villagers to explore how they could bring about change together.

Soldiers made travel increasingly more dangerous. They tortured or killed Indians caught helping Rigoberta or anyone who questioned the army. Sometimes they destroyed whole villages.

On Labor Day in 1981, Rigoberta slipped into Guatemala City with other CUC members. They passed out leaflets and blocked roads in front of the Spanish embassy. They wanted Guatemalans to remember the brave men who had died there.

By then, the army knew Rigoberta's name and face. When soldiers spotted her on the street, she barely escaped. Soon after, Rigoberta decided to leave Guatemala. Friends hid her in different safe houses and churches while they planned her getaway. After many weeks, she fled through the mountains and onto an airplane bound for Mexico.

Rigoberta Menchú arrived in Mexico City heartbroken. She felt like an outlaw for sneaking out of Guatemala, the only home she had ever known. Now at twenty-two, the lonely woman never expected to see any of her family alive again. Only two younger sisters were still alive for certain. Two brothers had disappeared and were believed to be dead.

Rigoberta still had no formal schooling and knew limited Spanish. She needed a job and a place to stay. More than anything, she longed to return and carry on her parents' work.

Members of a church group helped Rigoberta meet other refugees. Some refugees shared their overcrowded shacks. Wealthier people who respected Rigoberta's beliefs opened their homes and fed her. To repay the kindness, Rigoberta washed dishes and replaced the food whenever she could. She was grateful that strangers welcomed her and made her feel like part of a family.

Friends of CUC found odd jobs for Rigoberta. She had a small part in the movie *El Norte,* a film about Mayas who were forced to flee Guatemala. Most of her time, however, was spent uniting other Indians with Europeans who wanted to help them.

At first, few people knew much about Rigoberta. They thought of her as the daughter of Vicente Menchú, the CUC leader who had died for Indian rights in the Spanish embassy. Then, as more and more people got to know Rigoberta, they were struck by her clear mind and gentle voice. Rigoberta became known as a gifted speaker.

For the first time, Rigoberta met ladinos who accepted her as an equal. They worked side by side to end the silence about the Mayas' suffering in her homeland. One ladino man became a special friend. Rigoberta hungered for love and a simple life. But she worried about marrying.

Rigoberta appears in public wearing the designs of her village.
(Dick Bancroft)

"My main duty is to my people and then to my personal happiness," she said sadly.[14] The two parted for different countries and never saw each other again. For many years, Rigoberta led an unusual life for a Guatemalan woman. Marrying young and having many children was very important, especially to the Mayas.

Toward the end of 1981, Rigoberta Menchú toured the United States and Europe with other Guatemalans. She spoke with groups and tried to raise money to fight injustice in Guatemala. Audiences were touched by the way Rigoberta spoke about the many Guatemalans like herself who had fled the army but had done nothing wrong.

Two years later, Rigoberta was invited to the People's Tribunal in Madrid, Spain, a United Nations (UN) court composed of world leaders

Above left: By 1988, Rigoberta had built a new life for herself in Mexico City. (Marvin Collins)

Above right: Rigoberta met with reporters after receiving the 1992 Nobel Peace Prize. (UN Photo)

Below: In 1992, Rigoberta talked with Guatemalans who fled to El Porvenir, Mexico. (Kathleen Holloway)

seeking peace. Rigoberta told her powerful story in front of television cameras and a jury. The five-foot-tall, wide-eyed woman moved listeners to tears. Afterward, Rigoberta played the Mayan keeper of the fire with a Madrid theater group. She showed the world how Mayas respect their traditions.

The jury of ten noted human rights leaders urged the United Nations to open a human rights file on Guatemala. This meant that a group would check every year to ensure that Guatemala improved its human rights record. Rigoberta was hopeful. Noted peaceseekers at the People's Tribunal had listened.

Rigoberta decided that the United Nations was a good route to gain world attention for native peoples. From then on, she worked with many UN committees. Her colorful Quiché clothes became a common sight in the halls of UN buildings in New York and European cities.

Arturo Taracena, a Guatemalan who lived in France, heard Rigoberta speak. He arranged for her to talk with writer Elisabeth Burgos-Debray in Paris. Ms. Burgos-Debray turned Rigoberta's painful tale into the book *I, Rigoberta Menchú*.

The book was published in twelve languages, allowing many people to read about Rigoberta and Guatemala. Her story set the scene for *Guatemala: When the Mountains Tremble*, a film about the violent Guatemalan army. With this film, the voice of a poor, uneducated Maya led the call for Guatemalan human rights.

Rigoberta made a few trips to Guatemala. But each stop was cut short by government death threats. After her visits, Guatemalan soldiers attacked supporters within the country. They saw Rigoberta as a troublemaker. She was quickly gaining international attention and making the Guatemalan government look bad. Rigoberta now needed guards wherever she went, even at home in Mexico City.

Rigoberta traveled to many countries and met with their leaders. She talked with reporters. In one three-month period, she spoke to 310 groups. This hectic pace led to many awards from peace groups around the world.

But the killing and torture continued in Guatemala. The war between the army and the poor people who fought back had now claimed one hundred thousand lives. Another thirty thousand were reported missing, and two hundred thousand had fled to Mexico. Rigoberta and her friends searched in vain for something that would force change in Guatemala.

SIX

Dreams of Peace

An answer came when Nobel Peace Prize winners Bishop Desmond Tutu of South Africa and Adolfo Esquivel of Argentina suggested Rigoberta's name to the Nobel Committee. The five-member panel agreed that Rigoberta would be a good choice for the 1992 Nobel Peace Prize. "Rigoberta Menchú appeals to the best in all of us, wherever we live and whatever our background," they said.[15]

On December 10, 1992, Rigoberta flew to Stockholm, Sweden, to receive her gold medal and 1.2 million dollars. She accepted the prize with deep emotion in her voice. "I consider this prize, not as an award to me, but . . . for the human rights and for the rights of the indigenous [native] people. . . . "[16]

The Nobel Peace Prize unlocked many doors for Rigoberta. The United Nations secretary-general named her Goodwill Ambassador for the 1993 International Year of the World's Indigenous

Rigoberta addressed a 1993 human rights conference as Goodwill Ambassador for the International Year of the World's Indigenous (Native) People. (UN Photo)

People. Her struggle for native human rights now had the formal backing of a famous world group.

"My campaign is not for the Quiché Indians alone. It is for all native peoples," she repeated many times.[17]

Rigoberta used her prize money to start the Vicente Menchú Foundation, which helped native people improve their communities. She opened offices in Mexico City, where she still lived and worked with CUC, and in Guatemala City and Berkeley, California.

The foundation arranged the yearly Summit of Indigenous Peoples. About two hundred native and non-Indian world leaders attended each meeting. They focused on ways to teach poor people how to create better health care and schools. At the meetings, leaders also planned how to preserve native customs and educate non-Indians to respect them.

The Nobel Peace Prize created demand for Rigoberta around the world. In one week, she received five hundred invitations to speak. Rigoberta became a tireless traveler, returning to Mexico only four months out of the year. As a girl, Rigoberta never had a childhood. Now she never seemed to have a normal, simple life. At times, she longed for a home and family.

Rigoberta's earning the Nobel Peace Prize caused major shock waves inside Guatemala. Leaders spoke proudly of her work to reporters. In private they said that Rigoberta had shamed the country and should never have won the prize. The army launched new attacks to punish her followers.

Rigoberta still needed protection. Friends from other countries always stayed by her side to ensure her safety. Grave danger remained for her and her people, even with the world watching.

But the spotlight on Guatemala forced government leaders to soften their stand against change. Leaders began talks with Indian groups to end the constant fighting. With time, both sides welcomed Rigoberta's active role in these peace talks.

The first big breakthrough came three months after the Nobel Committee announced Rigoberta's prize. The government agreed to give land to Guatemalans in Mexico who wanted to return. In January 1993, Rigoberta led about twenty four hundred Indians into Guatemala.

Three months later Rigoberta met with government leaders to help select a new president. During the talks, someone recommended Rigoberta. The suggestion never went further. But the *thought* of a poor, uneducated Mayan woman as president of Guatemala was a big step forward!

When Rigoberta visits Guatemalans in their Mexican refugee camps, they talk about ways to bring about peace.
(Kathleen Holloway)

During the following years, Rigoberta visited different Indian groups and became their common leader. Government officials learned they could trust her calm manner and easy smile. Rigoberta managed to do what an entire war could not—give native people a voice in Guatemala and the world.

Rigoberta knew more work was needed before her people could gain equal rights. The new president, whom she helped to choose, claimed to want peace. Yet the army continued its violent attacks

Bodyguards protect Rigoberta in Guatemala. She continues to speak out on behalf of Mayans.
(Peace Brigades International)

against poor Guatemalans. More Indian families returned to their communities. But the government refused to give them land to resettle. Peace talks—and Rigoberta's role as a voice for her people—dragged on. One bright spot was Rigoberta's marriage to a man who shared her dream of peace.

Rigoberta often thought about her bittersweet life. The Nobel Peace Prize was a great gift for her people. Still, she would trade all of her awards for the return of her parents and the six brothers and sisters who she knew were dead. But Rigoberta remained hopeful.

"We have broken the silence around Guatemala," she said. "Now I would like to see native and non-native people living side by side. Maybe I won't live to see it but maybe others after me will."[18]

Endnotes

1. Burgos-Debray, Elisabeth. *I, Rigoberta Menchú: An Indian Woman in Guatemala* (New York: Verso, 1992), pp. 12–13.

2. Ibid., p. 28.

3. Ibid., p. 29.

4. Ibid., p. 31.

5. Ibid., p. 32.

6. Ibid., p. 31.

7. Ibid., p. 34.

8. Ibid., p. 41.

9. Ibid., p. 68.

10. Ibid., p. 94.

11. Ibid., p. 101.

12. Ibid., p. 114.

13. Ibid., p. 115.

14. Arias, Arturo, San Francisco State University. Telephone interview with author, 4 April 1994.

15. The Nobel Foundation, "Les Prix Nobel," 1992, p. 31. From speech delivered by Francis Sejersted, chair of the Norwegian Nobel Committee, Oslo, December 10, 1992.

16. Ibid., p. 170. Acceptance speech from Rigoberta Menchú Tum, Oslo, December 10, 1992.

17. United Nations, "International Year of the World's Indigenous People," 1993 student leaflet, p. 16.

18. Resource Center of the Americas, "Rigoberta Menchú: The Prize that Broke the Silence," 317-17th Avenue, Minneapolis, MN 55414-2077, 1993, p. 14.

Glossary

centavo a Guatemalan unit of money. One hundred centavos equals one quetzal.

fiesta celebration

finca plantation or large farm

huipil embroidered or woven blouse worn by Indian women

ladino Guatemalans who are either children of Mayan and Spanish parents or Mayas who reject Mayan dress, language, and customs

mimbre type of willow tree with branches that are good for making cane baskets and furniture

quetzal Guatemalan money that is divided into one hundred centavos

tamal maize paste wrapped in leaves from the maize or banana plant and cooked

tortilla pancake made from a dough of ground maize and water. Tortillas are a staple food of Guatemala.

Further Reading About Rigoberta Menchú, Guatemala, and the Search for Peace

Anglund, Joan Walsh. *Peace Is a Circle of Love*. New York: Gulliver Books, 1993. (nonfiction)

Cameron, Ann. *The Most Beautiful Place in the World*. New York: Knopf, 1988. (fiction)

Castañeda, Omar. *Abuela's Weave*. New York: Lee & Low Books, 1993. (fiction)

Cummins, Ronald. *Children of the World: Guatemala*. Milwaukee, Wis.: Gareth Stevens, 1990. (nonfiction)

Durell, Ann, and Marilyn Sachs, editors. *The Big Book for Peace*. New York: Dutton, 1990. (fiction)

For Older Readers

Acker, Alison. *Children of the Volcano*. Westport, Conn.: Lawrence Hill, 1986. (nonfiction)

Brill, Marlene Targ. *Guatemala*. Chicago: Childrens Press, 1993. (nonfiction)

Castañeda, Omar. *Among the Volcanoes*. New York: Lodestar Books, 1991. (fiction)

Castañeda, Omar. *Imagining Isabel*. New York: Lodestar Books, 1994. (fiction)

Index

Page numbers in *italics* refer to map and photographs.

Argentina, 41

Berkeley, California, 42
Burgos-Debray, Elisabeth, 39

Cakchiquel, 29
Catholic nuns, 29
centavos, 13, 18
Chimel, 7, 15, 17, 22, 27, 31
  attacks on, 25, 28
  fiesta in, 31
  home in, 4, 17
coffee picking, 5, 13–14, 18
  pay for, 13–14, 18, 19
Committee of Peasant Unity (CUC):
  forming of, 30
  on Labor Day, 1981, 34–35
  Rigoberta with, 33, 42
  at Spanish embassy, 32
customs, of Mayas:
  with animals, 16

at birth, 5–6
respect for, 6–7, 39

El Norte, 35
El Quiché province, 4
Esquivel, Adolfo, 41
Europeans, help from, 35, 39

farm store, 14
finca:
  bosses on, 12, 14
  death on, 15, 18
  definition of, 5
  living on, 12–13
  picking coffee on, 13–14
  ride to, 12
  sickness from, 14, 18–19
  uniting workers on, 34
food:
  on *fincas*, 13, 14
  as gifts from earth, 1–2
  lack of, 4, 8–10, 12, 15
  for meals, 7

Guatemala, 1, 35, 39, 40, 43
    human rights record in, 39
    Indians' return to, 44
    injustice in, 37
    map of, *viii*
    mountains of, 4
    reaction to Nobel prize in,
        43
Guatemala City, 42
    march in, 32
    Rigoberta in, 10, 19, 34–35,
        45
    Vicente Menchú Foundation
        in, 42–43
*Guatemala: When the Mountains
    Tremble* (film), 39
Guatemalan army, 1, 30, 37, 43
    attack on Spanish embassy, 32
    in village raids, 16, 25
    violence of, 28, 39, 40, 45–46

huipiles, 4, 20
human rights, 39, 42

I, Rigoberta Menchú (book), 39

judges, 15, 16, 17, 22, 30

ladinos, 11, 17, 36
    clothes of, 20
    laws of, 28
    treatment of Mayas by, 21–22
land, 4
    treasures from, 5–6
landowners, 4, 6, 14, 19, 22, 27
    in payoffs, 16–17, 24
    protests against, 15–17, 25

language, 11, 13, 15, 28–29
    see also Quiché, Spanish
        language
lawyers, 16

Madrid, Spain, 37, 39
maize, 7, 31
Mam, 29
Mayas, 1, 2, 17, 22, 35, 39
    children of, 11, 15, 37
    customs of, 5–6, 16, 19, 25
    fighting back by, 25–27, 32
    languages of, 11, 13, 15,
        28–29
    suffering of, 29, 36
    violence against, 1, 16, 25
Menchú, Juana (mother), 4, 5,
    7, 8, 14–15, 16, 19
    killing of, 32
    as maid, 23, 24
Menchú, Rigoberta:
    awards received by, 40, 46
    birth of, 5–6
    brothers and sisters of, 5, 7, 8,
        14–15, 23, 24, 30, 31–32, 46
    childhood jobs of, 7–8
    clothes of, 1, 7, 19, 20, 39
    as coffee picker, 13–14, 18
    collecting *mimbre*, 8–10
    on *finca*, 12–15, 18–19, 23
    as Goodwill Ambassador
        for the 1993 International
        Year of the World's
        Indigenous People,
        41–42, *42*
    in Guatemala City, 10–11,
        34–35, 42, *45*

as human rights speaker,
36–37, *38*, 39–40, 43
languages studied by, 19,
29
as maid, 19–22
marriage of, 46
in Mexico, 1, 35–36, *38*, 40
42, *44*
as Nobel Peace Prize
winner, 1–3, *2*, *38*,
41–43, 46
protection of, 35, 40, 43
return to Guatemala, 1–3, 40
jobs as young girl, 18
sadness of, 11, 15, 32–33
in United Nations, 39
as village leader, 24–25,
26–29
in village raids, 16
Menchú, Vicente (father), 4,
5, 9, 16, 19
as CUC founder, 30–31, 36
in Guatemala City, 10–11
in jail, 22–23, 30
kidnapping of, 24
killing of, 32
Rigoberta with, 8, 9–11,
18, 19
tricked by landowners,
16–17
as village leader, 8, 15–16
Mexico, 1, *38*, 40, 44, *44*
Vicente Menchú
Foundation in, 42–43
Mexico City, 35, *38*, 40, 42
mimbre:
definition of, 5

collection of, 8–10
sale of, 10–11

Native Americans, 3
New York City, 39
Nicolás (brother), 14
death of, 15
Nobel Committee, 41, 43
Nobel Peace Prize, 2, *2*,
41–42, 43

Paris, France, 39
peace talks, 43–46
People's Tribunal, 37–38
Petrocinio (brother), 7
killing of, 31–32

quetzals, 11, 19, 22
Quiché, 20
Indians, 42
language, 28

refugee camps, 35, *38*, *44*

San Juan, 23
San Marcos, Guatemala, 1, *2*
Spain, 6
Spanish embassy, 32, 34, 36
Spanish language:
of landowners, 11, 15, 28
of Rigoberta, 19, 20
Stockholm, Sweden, 41
Summit of Indigenous
Peoples, 42–43

Taracena, Arturo, 39
tortillas, making of, 7

Tutu, Bishop Desmond, 41
Tzutujil, 29

United Nations (UN), 37, 39
41–42

Vicente Menchú Foundation,
42–43
villages:
attacks on, 16, 28

leaders of, 5, 6, 15, 28
meetings in, 22
Rigoberta's role in, 18, 27

wages:
for picking coffee, 13–14,
18, 19
as maid, 19–20, 22
see also centavos, quetzals